HOW DOES THE FOOD CHAIN WORK?

SCIENCE BOOK FOR KIDS 9-12

Children's Science & Nature Books

BABY PROFESSOR
EDUCATION KIDS

Speedy Publishing LLC
40 E. Main St. #1156
Newark, DE 19711
www.speedypublishing.com

Have you ever wondered how plants and animals survive in the wild? We all know about watering and feeding plants and animals in your home, but how do they survive outside of the home? In this book, you will be learning the answers to those questions and more!

THE FOOD CHAIN AND THE FOOD WEB

Ecosystem Diagram

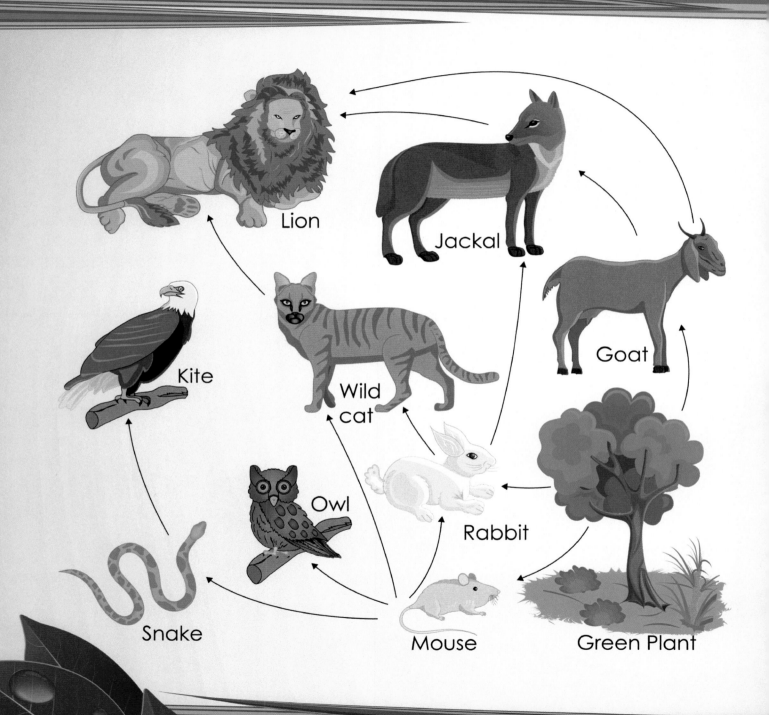

All living animals and plants need energy for survival. The sun, water, and soil provide energy for plants. Animals get their energy from plants as well as other animals for their energy.

As part of an ecosystem, animals and plants all depend upon one another to survive. Scientists often refer to this dependence as the food chain or the food web.

Illustration of food web.

WHAT IS A FOOD CHAIN?

The way the different types of organisms obtain their energy by eating each other is known as the food chain, beginning with the plant and ending with the animal. An example of how you would describe the lion's food chain would be like this -- the lion eats the antelope and the antelope eats grass, which can be drawn like this: grass-->antelope-->lion.

Lion Hunting Zebra.

LINKS OF THE CHAIN

Each link of the food chain is described by its name, and mostly depend upon what an organism eats and how it then contributes to the ecosystem energy cycle.

Frog Catching Cricket with Tongue.

PRODUCERS - The plants are producers since they produce the energy for our ecosystem. They are able to do so since they absorb energy from the sun by photosynthesis. We will be discussing photosynthesis later in the book. In addition, they need to have water and nutrients from the soil, however, plants are the only way new energy is created.

Moss

CONSUMERS – The animals are the consumers since they do not produce energy, they just use it. They are referred to as herbivores or primary consumers. Carnivores, or secondary consumers, are animals that eat other animals. A tertiary consumer is a carnivore that eats another carnivore. There are some animals that eat both animals and plants. They are referred to as omnivores.

A Springbok Eating Flowers.

DECOMPOSERS - Organisms that eat decaying matter such as dead animals or plants are referred to as decomposers. Decomposers put the nutrients back into the ground and soil for the plants to eat. Fungi, bacteria, and worms are examples of decomposers.

Earthworm in Damp Soil.

Returning to the previous example:

Grass ---> Antelope ---> Lion

Producer = Grass

Primary Consumer = Antelope

Secondary Consumer = Lion

Lion in High Grass.

LOST ENERGY

As mentioned earlier, all of the energy created in the food chain originates from the plants, or producers, which convert the sunlight to energy by photosynthesis. The remaining food chain simply uses the energy which results in the loss of energy as you move down the food chain. Because of this, less organisms are available the further you get down the food chain.

Food chain, ecosystem connections.

Solar energy

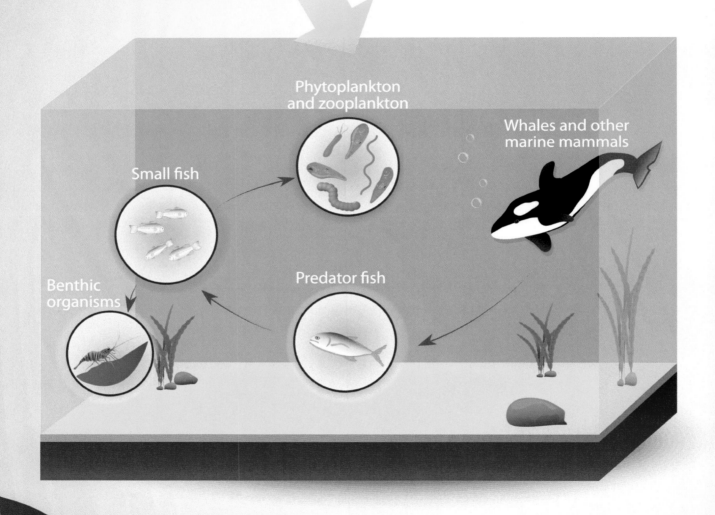

Again, looking at our example earlier, there is more grass than antelope, and more antelope than lions. The antelope and lions use the energy up when they do stuff like breathing, running, and hunting.

Marine Food Web Diagram shows the relationships among organisms living in ocean. producers and consumers: tuna, killer whale, shrimps and plankton.

EACH LINK PLAYS AN IMPORTANT ROLE

The links that are higher up in the chain rely upon the links that are lower in the food chain. While lions do not eat grass, they would not be able to survive long if there was not any grass since the antelope would not have anything to eat.

Stalking Lions.

THE FOOD WEB

There are several food chains in any ecosystem. Typically, most animals and plants have a role in several chains. When you combine all of these chains the result is known as the food web.

Baltimore Oriole

WHAT ARE THE TROPHIC LEVELS

The organisms found in the food chains are categorized into trophic levels. These levels are then divided into the producers, which are the first trophic level; consumers, which are the second, third, and fourth levels; and the decomposers.

SIMPLIFIED GRAZING TROPHIC CHAIN

GREEN PLANTS   PRIMARY PRODUCERS

HERBIVOROUS PRIMARY CONSUMERS

 SECONDARY CONSUMERS

CARNIVORES  TERTIARY CONSUMERS

 QUATERNARY CONSUMERS

Producers, which are also referred to as autotrophs, create their own food and they are the first level of all food chains. They are typically one-celled organisms or plants. Most all of them use photosynthesis for creating food from sunlight, water and carbon dioxide.

Food Chain

The second level is comprised of the organisms that eat the producers, and are also known as herbivores, or primary consumers. Turtles, deer, and several species of birds are known to be herbivores. The herbivores are eaten by the secondary consumers and the they are eaten by the tertiary consumers. There is a possibility that more levels of consumers exist before the chain finally gets to its top predator. Also known as apex predators, top predators eat other consumers.

Sea Turtle Feeding.

Consumers may be carnivores, which are animals that eat other animals; or omnivores, which are animals that eat both animals and plants. Like people, omnivores consume many different types of food. People eat plants, including fruits and vegetables, as well as animals and animal products, including eggs, milk and meat. We also eat mushrooms, which is fungi.

Wild Mushroom

The final part of the food chains are decomposers and detritivores. Organisms that eat nonliving animals and plant remains are detritivores. An example would be scavengers which includes vultures that eat dead animals and dung beetles that eat animal feces.

Griffin Vultures

WHAT ARE THE TROPHIC LEVELS

Have you noticed that plants have to have sunlight in order to live? Does that seem strange to you? How is sunlight considered to be food? The answer to that is sunlight provides energy as well as the process that plants use to absorb the energy from the sunlight and convert the carbon dioxide and the water into food.

WHAT ARE THE THREE THINGS THAT PLANTS NEED TO LIVE?

The three basic things that plants need to live are sunlight, water, and carbon dioxide. They breathe the carbon dioxide the same way we breathe oxygen. As they breathe in the carbon dioxide, they then breathe out oxygen. Plants are the greatest source of oxygen on Earth and help to keep us alive.

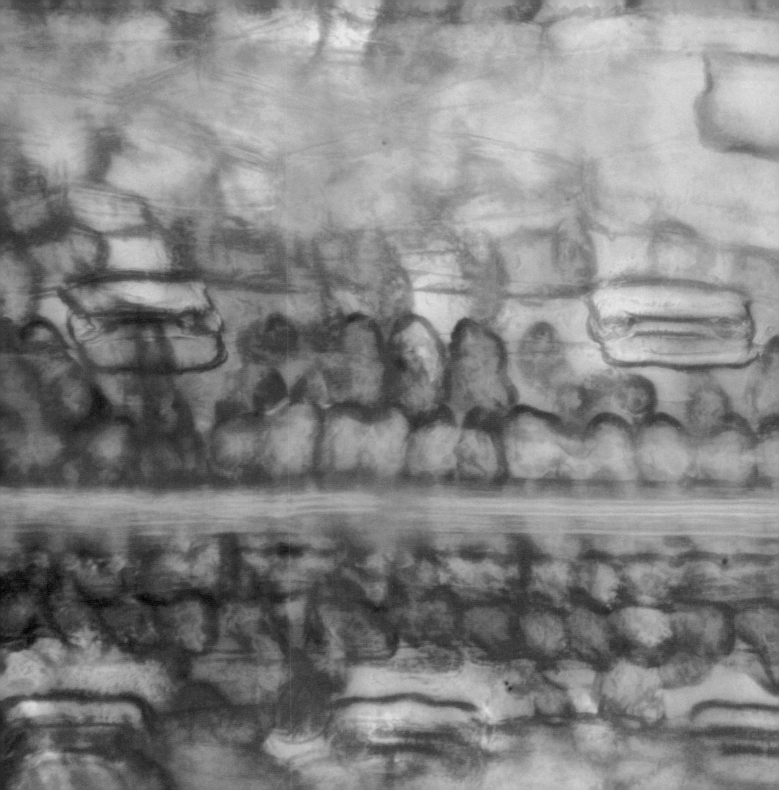

So, we now know that they use sunlight for energy, they get their water from the rain, and they receive carbon dioxide by breathing. Photosynthesis is the process of putting these three main ingredients together and creating food.

Leaf Under a Microscope.

HOW DO THEY CAPTURE SUNLIGHT?

Plants are able to capture sunlight by using a compound known as chlorophyll, which is green, and that is why plants are green. You might initially think that its green since it wants to absorb and utilize green light, however, we know that the color we actually see is the color of light which is reflected. Consequently, chlorophyll does actually reflect green light and absorbs red and blue light.

The Sun.

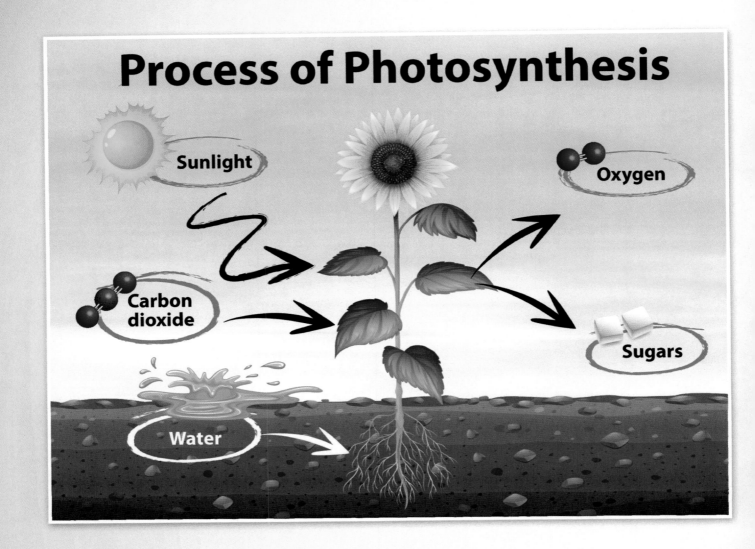

MORE ABOUT PHOTOSYNTHESIS

Chloroplasts are structures located inside a plant's cells and this is where you will find chlorophyll.

The photosynthesis process has two main stages. During the first phase, the chloroplasts capture the sunlight and the energy is then stored using a chemical called APT. During the second phase, ATP is then used for creating sugar and organic compounds. These are foods that plants utilize to grow and live.

Sunlight is required for the first phase. However, the second phase does not require sunlight and can even occur at night. The second phase is referred to as the Calvin Cycle since it was discovered by a scientist known as Melvin Calvin.

PROCESS OF PHOTOSYNTHESIS

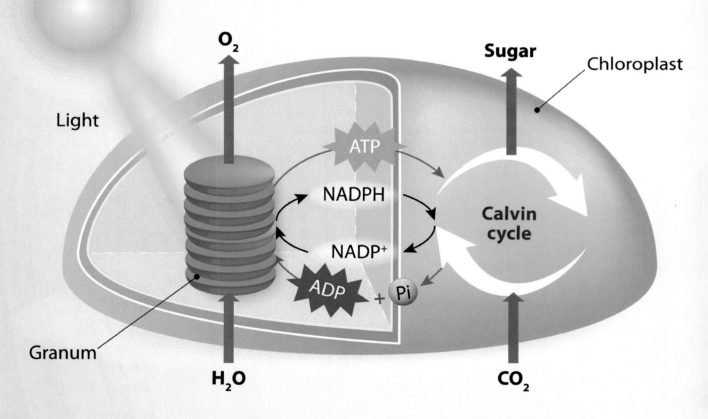

Diagram of the process of photosynthesis, showing the light reactions and the Calvin cycle.

Even though they must have water and sunlight to survive, different species of plants require different amounts of each. Some types of plants require just a little bit of water, while other types might need a lot more. Some like to be in direct sunlight all day long, and others might prefer shade. Learning about the requirements of plants can help you to learn where to plant them and how much water they need to flourish.

SUMMARY

We now know that plants require water, sunlight, and carbon dioxide to survive. They take these components and with the use of chlorophyll are able to make them into food, which they then use for energy, as well as oxygen, which they breathe out and we then use the oxygen for survival.

Photosynthesis Diagram.

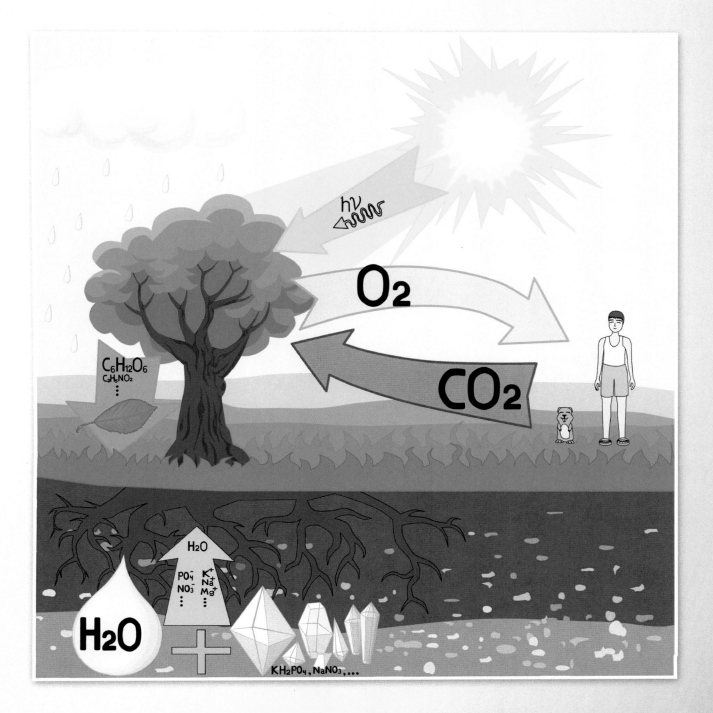

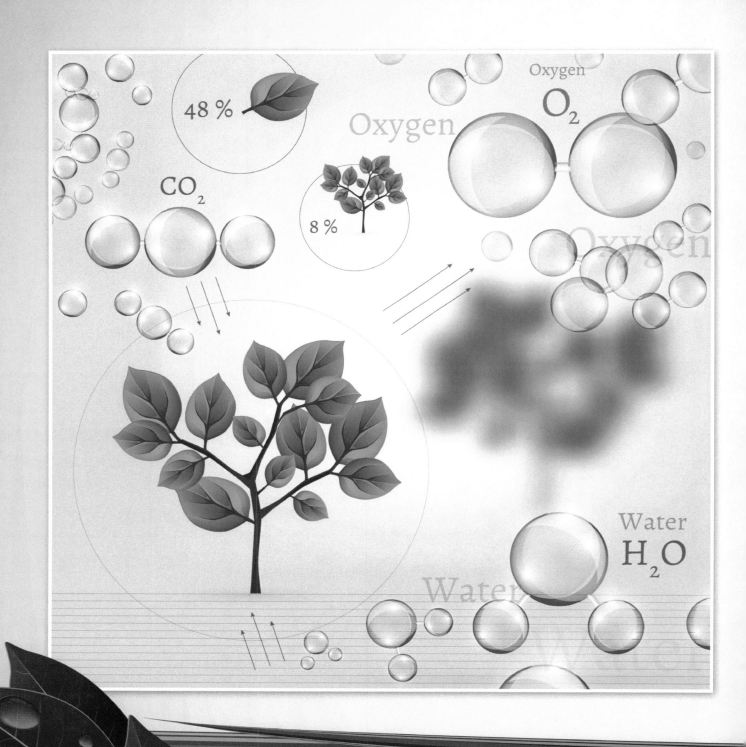

THE OXYGEN CYCLE

Oxygen is a vital element to our precious life on planet Earth and is the greatest common element of our body. Approximately 65% of the mass of our bodies consists of oxygen. Most of it is in the form of water. It also makes up approximately 20% of the atmosphere and 30% of Earth is comprised of oxygen.

Ecology set with oxygen, water and carbon dioxide molecules.

WHAT IS THE OXYGEN CYCLE?

Oxygen is always being utilized and made by many different processes on Earth. Together, all of these processes make the oxygen cycle. It is interconnected with the carbon cycle.

BREATHING – Respiration is the scientific name for breathing. All plants and animals use it as they breathe, breathing in oxygen and breathing out carbon dioxide.

Oxygen Bubbles

WHAT PROCESSES USE OXYGEN?

DECOMPOSING – Once animals and plants die, they then decompose and this process utilizes oxygen and releases carbon dioxide.

RUSTING – Rusting is also known as oxidation. As items rust, they utilize oxygen.

COMBUSTION – The three items needed for fire are heat, oxygen and fuel. If there is no oxygen, there will be no fire. As things burn, they use up the oxygen and then replace it with carbon dioxide.

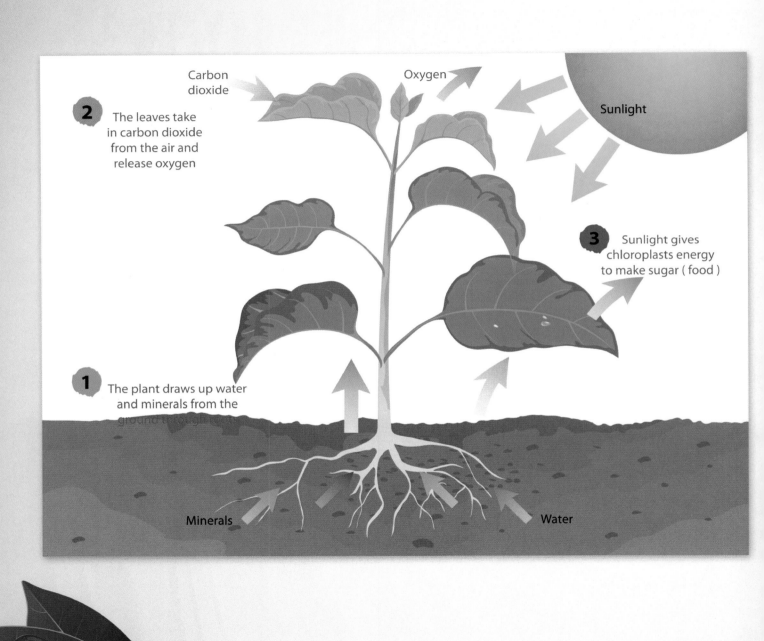

WHAT PROCESSES PRODUCE OXYGEN

PLANTS – The majority of the oxygen we breathe is created by a process known as photosynthesis. Plants utilize carbon dioxide, water, and sunlight for creating energy for this process. They also are able to create oxygen which is released into the air.

Photosynthesis. This is the process by which most plants make food using sunlight.

The food chain is a necessary part of our ecosystem. The next time you see a beautiful flower, think about how the food chain works for it to survive.

For additional about the food chain, the food web, photosynthesis or the oxygen cycle, you can go to your local library, research the internet, and ask questions of your teachers, family and friends.

The hierarchy of biological organization.

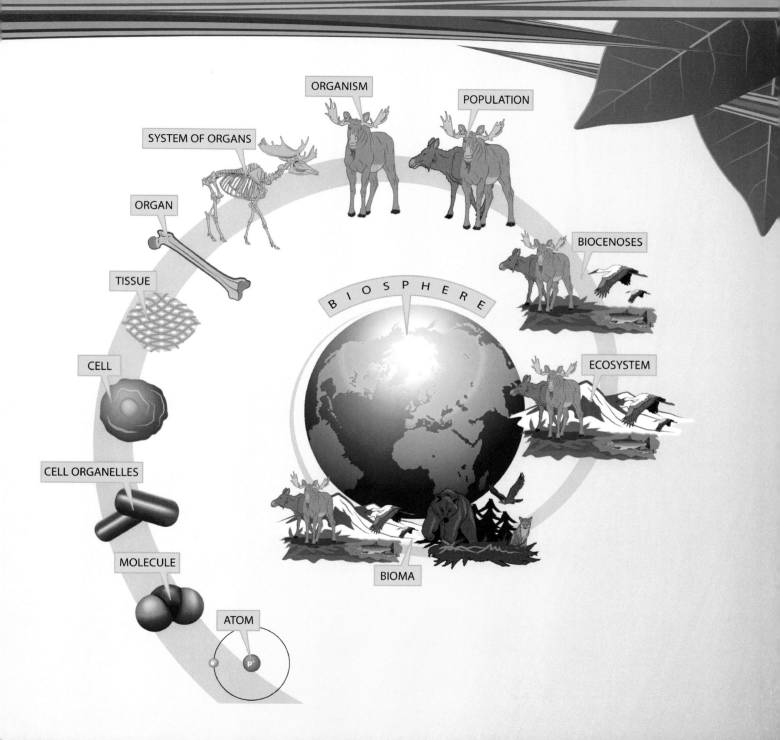

Made in the USA
Monee, IL
09 February 2024